Budget / Finance Planner

Cape Turnaround™ Planners

Budget / Finance Planner (Weekly/Monthly)

Send Questions & Inquiries to info@capeturnaround.com

This Planner Belongs to:

Name: ______________________________

Address: ______________________________

____

Phone: ______________________________

E-mail: ______________________________

Savings Tracker

Beginning Balance	

Date	Deposit/Draw	Balance

Goals

Goals

Goals

Notes

Savings Tracker

Beginning Balance	

Date	Deposit/Draw	Balance

Goals

Goals

Goals

Notes

Debt Tracker

Debt #1	
Beginning Balance	
Minimum Payment Due	

Date Paid	Amount Paid	Current Balance

Debt #3	
Beginning Balance	
Minimum Payment Due	

Date Paid	Amount Paid	Current Balance

Debt #2	
Beginning Balance	
Minimum Payment Due	

Date Paid	Amount Paid	Current Balance

Debt #4	
Beginning Balance	
Minimum Payment Due	

Date Paid	Amount Paid	Current Balance

Notes

Debt Tracker

Debt #5	
Beginning Balance	
Minimum Payment Due	

Date Paid	Amount Paid	Current Balance

Debt #7	
Beginning Balance	
Minimum Payment Due	

Date Paid	Amount Paid	Current Balance

Debt #6	
Beginning Balance	
Minimum Payment Due	

Date Paid	Amount Paid	Current Balance

Debt #8	
Beginning Balance	
Minimum Payment Due	

Date Paid	Amount Paid	Current Balance

Notes

Debt Tracker

Debt #9	
Beginning Balance	
Minimum Payment Due	

Date Paid	Amount Paid	Current Balance

Debt #11	
Beginning Balance	
Minimum Payment Due	

Date Paid	Amount Paid	Current Balance

Debt #10	
Beginning Balance	
Minimum Payment Due	

Date Paid	Amount Paid	Current Balance

Debt #12	
Beginning Balance	
Minimum Payment Due	

Date Paid	Amount Paid	Current Balance

Notes

Debt Tracker

Debt #5	
Beginning Balance	
Minimum Payment Due	

Date Paid	Amount Paid	Current Balance

Debt #7	
Beginning Balance	
Minimum Payment Due	

Date Paid	Amount Paid	Current Balance

Debt #6	
Beginning Balance	
Minimum Payment Due	

Date Paid	Amount Paid	Current Balance

Debt #8	
Beginning Balance	
Minimum Payment Due	

Date Paid	Amount Paid	Current Balance

Notes

Goals for the Month

Month ______________________

Mon	Tues	Wed	Thurs	Fri	Sat	Sun

Monthly Budget

Income		
Source	Budgeted	Actual
Total		

Savings/Reserves	
Amount	Account Deposited
Total	

Bill	Due Date	Amount Due	Amount Paid	Comments

Notes

Expense Tracker

Week 1

Description	Category	Date Paid	Amount

Week 2

Description	Category	Date Paid	Amount

Expense Tracker

Week 3

Description	Category	Date Paid	Amount

Week 4

Description	Category	Date Paid	Amount

Expense Tracker

Week 5

Description	Category	Date Paid	Amount

Notes

Monthly Budget Review

Income	
Expenses	
Savings	
Misc	
Net Balance	

Summary of Goals Met / Budget Wins

What did not work? / Plans for Improvement

Notes

Goals for the Month

Month ______________________________

Mon	Tues	Wed	Thurs	Fri	Sat	Sun

Monthly Budget

Income		
Source	Budgeted	Actual
Total		

Savings/Reserves	
Amount	Account Deposited
Total	

Bill	Due Date	Amount Due	Amount Paid	Comments

Notes

Expense Tracker

Week 1

Description	Category	Date Paid	Amount

Week 2

Description	Category	Date Paid	Amount

Expense Tracker

Week 3

Description	Category	Date Paid	Amount

Week 4

Description	Category	Date Paid	Amount

Expense Tracker

Week 5

Description	Category	Date Paid	Amount

Notes

Monthly Budget Review

Income	
Expenses	
Savings	
Misc	
Net Balance	

Summary of Goals Met / Budget Wins

What did not work? / Plans for Improvement

Notes

Goals for the Month

Month

Mon	Tues	Wed	Thurs	Fri	Sat	Sun

Monthly Budget

Income		
Source	Budgeted	Actual
Total		

Savings/Reserves	
Amount	Account Deposited
Total	

Bill	Due Date	Amount Due	Amount Paid	Comments

Notes

Expense Tracker

Week 1

Description	Category	Date Paid	Amount

Week 2

Description	Category	Date Paid	Amount

Expense Tracker

Week 3

Description	Category	Date Paid	Amount

Week 4

Description	Category	Date Paid	Amount

Expense Tracker

Week 5

Description	Category	Date Paid	Amount

Notes

Monthly Budget Review

Income	
Expenses	
Savings	
Misc	
Net Balance	

Summary of Goals Met / Budget Wins

What did not work? / Plans for Improvement

Notes

Goals for the Month

Month ____________________

Mon	Tues	Wed	Thurs	Fri	Sat	Sun

Monthly Budget

Income		
Source	Budgeted	Actual
Total		

Savings/Reserves	
Amount	Account Deposited
Total	

Bill	Due Date	Amount Due	Amount Paid	Comments

Notes

Expense Tracker

Week 1

Description	Category	Date Paid	Amount

Week 2

Description	Category	Date Paid	Amount

Expense Tracker

Week 3

Description	Category	Date Paid	Amount

Week 4

Description	Category	Date Paid	Amount

Expense Tracker

Week 5

Description	Category	Date Paid	Amount

Notes

Monthly Budget Review

Income	
Expenses	
Savings	
Misc	
Net Balance	

Summary of Goals Met | Budget Wins

What did not work? | Plans for Improvement

Notes

Goals for the Month

Month ______________________

Mon	Tues	Wed	Thurs	Fri	Sat	Sun

Monthly Budget

Income

Source	Budgeted	Actual
Total		

Savings/Reserves

Amount	Account Deposited
Total	

Bill	Due Date	Amount Due	Amount Paid	Comments

Notes

Expense Tracker

Week 1

Description	Category	Date Paid	Amount

Week 2

Description	Category	Date Paid	Amount

Expense Tracker

Week 3

Description	Category	Date Paid	Amount

Week 4

Description	Category	Date Paid	Amount

Expense Tracker

Week 5

Description	Category	Date Paid	Amount

Notes

Monthly Budget Review

Income	
Expenses	
Savings	
Misc	
Net Balance	

Summary of Goals Met / Budget Wins

What did not work? / Plans for Improvement

Notes

Goals for the Month

Month ____________________

Mon	Tues	Wed	Thurs	Fri	Sat	Sun

Monthly Budget

Income		
Source	Budgeted	Actual
Total		

Savings/Reserves	
Amount	Account Deposited
Total	

Bill	Due Date	Amount Due	Amount Paid	Comments

Notes

Expense Tracker

Week 1

Description	Category	Date Paid	Amount

Week 2

Description	Category	Date Paid	Amount

Expense Tracker

Week 3

Description	Category	Date Paid	Amount

Week 4

Description	Category	Date Paid	Amount

Expense Tracker

Week 5

Description	Category	Date Paid	Amount

Notes

Monthly Budget Review

Income	
Expenses	
Savings	
Misc	
Net Balance	

Summary of Goals Met / Budget Wins

What did not work? / Plans for Improvement

Notes

Goals for the Month

Month ______________________

Mon	Tues	Wed	Thurs	Fri	Sat	Sun

Monthly Budget

Income		
Source	Budgeted	Actual
Total		

Savings/Reserves	
Amount	Account Deposited
Total	

Bill	Due Date	Amount Due	Amount Paid	Comments

Notes

Expense Tracker

Week 1

Description	Category	Date Paid	Amount

Week 2

Description	Category	Date Paid	Amount

Expense Tracker

Week 3

Description	Category	Date Paid	Amount

Week 4

Description	Category	Date Paid	Amount

Expense Tracker

Week 5

Description	Category	Date Paid	Amount

Notes

Monthly Budget Review

Income	
Expenses	
Savings	
Misc	
Net Balance	

Summary of Goals Met / Budget Wins

What did not work? / Plans for Improvement

Notes

Goals for the Month

Month ____________________

Mon	Tues	Wed	Thurs	Fri	Sat	Sun

Monthly Budget

Income		
Source	Budgeted	Actual
Total		

Savings/Reserves	
Amount	Account Deposited
Total	

Bill	Due Date	Amount Due	Amount Paid	Comments

Notes

Expense Tracker

Week 1

Description	Category	Date Paid	Amount

Week 2

Description	Category	Date Paid	Amount

Expense Tracker

Week 3

Description	Category	Date Paid	Amount

Week 4

Description	Category	Date Paid	Amount

Expense Tracker

Week 5

Description	Category	Date Paid	Amount

Notes

Monthly Budget Review

Income	
Expenses	
Savings	
Misc	
Net Balance	

Summary of Goals Met / Budget Wins

What did not work? / Plans for Improvement

Notes

Goals for the Month

Month ____________________

Mon	Tues	Wed	Thurs	Fri	Sat	Sun

Monthly Budget

Income		
Source	Budgeted	Actual
Total		

Savings/Reserves	
Amount	Account Deposited
Total	

Bill	Due Date	Amount Due	Amount Paid	Comments

Notes

Expense Tracker

Week 1

Description	Category	Date Paid	Amount

Week 2

Description	Category	Date Paid	Amount

Expense Tracker

Week 3

Description	Category	Date Paid	Amount

Week 4

Description	Category	Date Paid	Amount

Expense Tracker

Week 5

Description	Category	Date Paid	Amount

Notes

Monthly Budget Review

Income	
Expenses	
Savings	
Misc	
Net Balance	

Summary of Goals Met / Budget Wins

What did not work? / Plans for Improvement

Notes

Goals for the Month

Month ______________________________

Mon	Tues	Wed	Thurs	Fri	Sat	Sun

Monthly Budget

Income		
Source	Budgeted	Actual
Total		

Savings/Reserves	
Amount	Account Deposited
Total	

Bill	Due Date	Amount Due	Amount Paid	Comments

Notes

Expense Tracker

Week 1

Description	Category	Date Paid	Amount

Week 2

Description	Category	Date Paid	Amount

Expense Tracker

Week 3

Description	Category	Date Paid	Amount

Week 4

Description	Category	Date Paid	Amount

Expense Tracker

Week 5

Description	Category	Date Paid	Amount

Notes

Monthly Budget Review

Income	
Expenses	
Savings	
Misc	
Net Balance	

Summary of Goals Met / Budget Wins

What did not work? / Plans for Improvement

Notes

Goals for the Month

Month ____________________

Mon	Tues	Wed	Thurs	Fri	Sat	Sun

Monthly Budget

Income		
Source	Budgeted	Actual
Total		

Savings/Reserves	
Amount	Account Deposited
Total	

Bill	Due Date	Amount Due	Amount Paid	Comments

Notes

Expense Tracker

Week 1

Description	Category	Date Paid	Amount

Week 2

Description	Category	Date Paid	Amount

Expense Tracker

Week 3

Description	Category	Date Paid	Amount

Week 4

Description	Category	Date Paid	Amount

Expense Tracker

Week 5

Description	Category	Date Paid	Amount

Notes

Monthly Budget Review

Income	
Expenses	
Savings	
Misc	
Net Balance	

Summary of Goals Met / Budget Wins

What did not work? / Plans for Improvement

Notes

Goals for the Month

Month ______________________

Mon	Tues	Wed	Thurs	Fri	Sat	Sun

Monthly Budget

Income		
Source	Budgeted	Actual
Total		

Savings/Reserves	
Amount	Account Deposited
Total	

Bill	Due Date	Amount Due	Amount Paid	Comments

Notes

Expense Tracker

Week 1

Description	Category	Date Paid	Amount

Week 2

Description	Category	Date Paid	Amount

Expense Tracker

Week 3

Description	Category	Date Paid	Amount

Week 4

Description	Category	Date Paid	Amount

Expense Tracker

Week 5

Description	Category	Date Paid	Amount

Notes

Monthly Budget Review

Income	
Expenses	
Savings	
Misc	
Net Balance	

Summary of Goals Met / Budget Wins

What did not work? / Plans for Improvement

Notes

Goals for the Month

Month ____________________

Mon	Tues	Wed	Thurs	Fri	Sat	Sun

Monthly Budget

Income		
Source	Budgeted	Actual
Total		

Savings/Reserves	
Amount	Account Deposited
Total	

Bill	Due Date	Amount Due	Amount Paid	Comments

Notes

Expense Tracker

Week 1

Description	Category	Date Paid	Amount

Week 2

Description	Category	Date Paid	Amount

Expense Tracker

Week 3

Description	Category	Date Paid	Amount

Week 4

Description	Category	Date Paid	Amount

Expense Tracker

Week 5

Description	Category	Date Paid	Amount

Notes

Monthly Budget Review

Income	
Expenses	
Savings	
Misc	
Net Balance	

Summary of Goals Met / Budget Wins

What did not work? / Plans for Improvement

Notes

Goals for the Month

Month ______________________________

Mon	Tues	Wed	Thurs	Fri	Sat	Sun

Monthly Budget

Income		
Source	Budgeted	Actual
Total		

Savings/Reserves	
Amount	Account Deposited
Total	

Bill	Due Date	Amount Due	Amount Paid	Comments

Notes

Expense Tracker

Week 1

Description	Category	Date Paid	Amount

Week 2

Description	Category	Date Paid	Amount

Expense Tracker

Week 3

Description	Category	Date Paid	Amount

Week 4

Description	Category	Date Paid	Amount

Expense Tracker

Week 5

Description	Category	Date Paid	Amount

Notes

Monthly Budget Review

Income	
Expenses	
Savings	
Misc	
Net Balance	

Summary of Goals Met / Budget Wins

What did not work? / Plans for Improvement

Notes

Christmas Budget

Notes

Notes

Christmas Budget

Group	Budgeted	Actual
Total		

Item	Budget	Actual	Comments

Total

Made in the USA
Monee, IL
08 November 2026

68002506R00063